P9-DTN-426

THE LIFE CYCLE OF A
POLAR BEAR
By Robin Merritt

Published by The Child's World®
1980 Lookout Drive
Mankato, MN 56003-1705
800-599-READ
www.childsworld.com

The Child's World®: Mary Berendes, Publishing Director
The Design Lab: Kathleen Petelinsek, design
Red Line Editorial: Editorial direction

Photographs ©: Till Von Au/123RF, cover (top left), 1 (top left); Keith Levit/Shutterstock Images, cover (top right, bottom left, bottom right), 1 (top right, bottom left, bottom right), 3; Shutterstock Images, 5, 25, 30; John Pitcher/iStockphoto, 6, 21, 31 (top); Jan Martin Will/Shutterstock Images, 9; Bruce Lichtenberger/iStockphoto, 10; AP Images, 13, 31 (bottom); Bev McConnell/iStockphoto, 14; Stefan Redel/iStockphoto, 17; Peter Zwitser/iStockphoto, 18; Witold Kaszkin/Shutterstock Images, 22; Thorsten Milse/Photolibrary, 26; Sergey Skleznev/Shutterstock Images, 29

ISBN: 978-1-60973-190-8
LCCN: 2011927740

Printed in the United States of America
Mankato, MN
July 2011
PA02089

CONTENTS

LIFE CYCLES

Every living thing has a life cycle. A life cycle is the steps a living thing goes through as it grows and changes. Humans have a life cycle. Animals have a life cycle. Plants have a life cycle, too.

A cycle is something that happens over and over again. A life cycle begins with the start of a new life. It continues as a plant or creature grows. And it keeps going as one living thing creates another, or **reproduces**—and the cycle starts over again.

A polar bear's life cycle has three main steps: **embryo**, cub, and adult polar bear.

After they are born, polar bears grow from cuddly cubs to strong adults.

Polar bears have thick fur that helps them stay warm in the icy north.

POLAR BEARS

Polar bears are among the biggest of all bears. They are **predators**, which means they hunt and eat other animals. Polar bears mainly eat seals, but they also feed on beluga whales, birds, and even walruses. They catch and kill their **prey** with their sharp teeth and claws.

Polar bears are **mammals**. Like people and other animals in this group, polar bears are warm-blooded. They keep a steady body temperature in hot or cold weather. Mammals also have fur or hair. Female mammals give birth to live babies instead of laying eggs. These mothers make milk to feed, or **nurse**, their young.

Polar bears live in the Arctic, the icy land and waters around the North Pole. The coldest parts of Alaska, Canada, Greenland, Norway, and Russia are all home to polar bears. But the bears spend most of their time on the sea ice at the top of the world.

Polar bears have the perfect bodies for frigid weather. They have layers of protection from the wind and cold. The top layer is thick fur that repels water and traps warm air. Underneath this fur their skin is black. Their black skin absorbs, or takes in, the heat from sunlight. And below this skin is a thick layer of fat called **blubber**. Like a heavy sleeping bag, blubber keeps bears toasty in the worst storms.

Polar bears live in some of the world's coldest places.

A **den** is a safe place for the mother to give birth to her cubs.

CUBS ARE BORN

Polar bear cubs are born in the middle of winter. The cubs have been growing inside their mother for six to nine months. The mother gives birth in a den she dug under the snow. The den is dark and warm.

Polar bear mothers usually give birth to twins. At birth, polar bear cubs are about the size of guinea pigs. The helpless infants cannot see. With only a little fine fur, they must snuggle into their mother's fur to keep warm. She licks her cubs and nurses them with her rich milk.

The cubs' eyes open, and the cubs grow stronger and furrier. Their mother feeds and guards them. She never leaves the den, even to eat. By early spring, the cubs each weigh more than 20 pounds (9 kg) and are about the size of cocker spaniel dogs.

Some polar bear cubs are born in zoos. Zoo workers help take care of them.

Polar bear cubs stay close to their mother when they leave the den.

INTO THE SUNSHINE

In the spring, the cubs are ready to leave the den. Their mother punches a hole in the snow, and they all climb out into the sunshine. The curious cubs play and explore in the snow, but they do not stray far from their mother. Their mother protects them from danger. But sometimes young cubs are killed by wolves or other bears.

By the time the mother bear leaves the den, she is starving! She has lost hundreds of pounds in her winter den. As soon as the cubs are strong enough, their mother teaches them to hunt.

HUNTING ON ICE

Polar bears are excellent hunters. Their fur works like **camouflage**, helping them blend into the snow. Hidden, they can sneak up on their prey for a surprise attack. Huge, furry paws help them travel far. Extra skin between their toes helps them swim for hours.

Ringed seals are polar bears' favorite food. In spring, mother seals and their pups can be found in icy dens. Polar bears can smell the seals inside. Mother polar bears lead their cubs and show them how to break inside the den. The bears eat as many seals as they can catch.

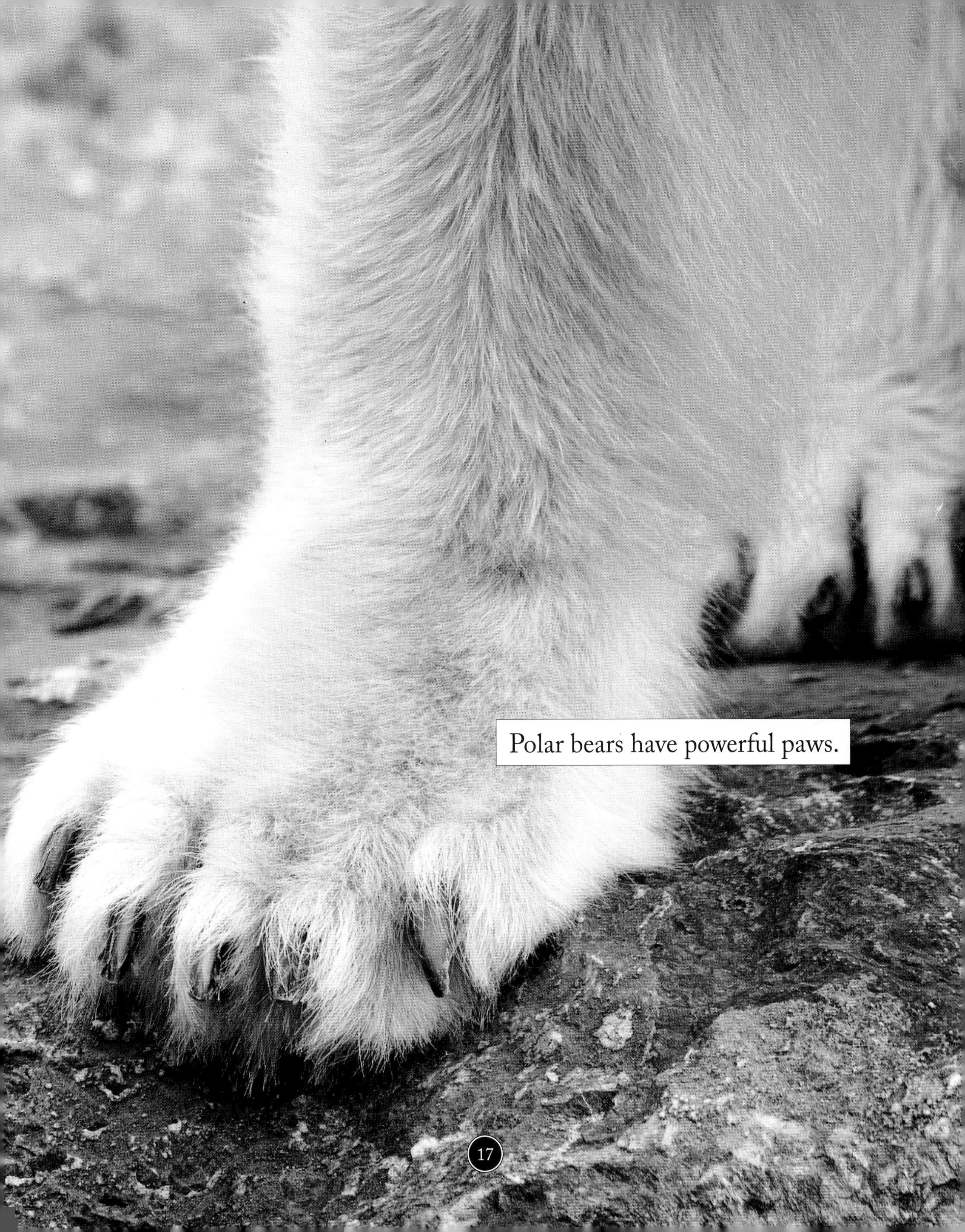

Polar bears have powerful paws.

Cubs learn to hunt for seals with their mother.

By summer, the ice melts and the seal pups can swim away. There is little meat for the bears. The hungry mother catches birds and eats eggs if she can find them. If she is strong, she can still nurse her cubs. But hunger kills many polar bears, young and old.

In fall, the seas freeze and there is more food again. The cubs are strong now and can follow their mother onto the sea ice. There, they learn to look for holes where seals come up for a breath of air. The mother bear teaches them how to sit for hours and hours, waiting for a seal. Then—whack! She slashes the seal with her strong paw and drags it out of the water for a family feast.

GROWING UP

The family stays together for about two years. Then the young bears can feed themselves, and the mother and cubs part forever.

The young polar bears continue to grow. A male polar bear can grow to weigh more than 1,300 pounds (590 kg). That's as much as a dairy cow! A female will grow to weigh about 550 pounds (250 kg).

Young cubs must learn to hunt before they can live on their own.

As an adult, a polar bear travels many miles looking for food.

In the wild, polar bears can live for about 30 years. Adult polar bears usually spend most of their time alone. They do not defend one area or stay in one place. Instead, they roam mile after mile, hunting for food. Despite their huge size, polar bears can chase prey at 25 miles per hour (40 kmh).

A POLAR BEAR PAIR

Female polar bears can have their own cubs by about age four or five. Males fight each other to win mates. They are often eight or nine before they are big enough to beat other males.

In spring, male polar bears look for mates. Several might follow one female for days. The males battle to win the female. The winning male spends about a week with the female. They play, rolling and jumping in the snow, and mate. After mating, they separate.

A **pregnant** female hunts and eats a lot. She needs energy for the embryos inside her. And she needs to store up fat, too.

In zoos, female polar bears are watched closely for signs that they might be pregnant. Some zoos make special dens for pregnant females.

In late fall, pregnant female polar bears enter their dens. They come out in spring with their cubs.

A WINTER CAVE

Male polar bears keep hunting all winter long. But in late fall, pregnant females dig their snowy dens. They will not leave their dens until March or April.

Black bears spend much of the winter in **hibernation**. This is a sleep so deep that breathing slows and body temperature falls. A pregnant polar bear does not really hibernate, but she does sleep on and off in her den. Her body temperature only drops a few degrees. Her warm body heats the den while the unborn cubs grow.

THE LIFE CYCLE GOES ON

In January, the Arctic is dark both day and night. The wind howls and snow flies. But inside a warm den, the female is nursing newborn cubs. The polar bear life cycle goes on.

A young cub plays with its mother.

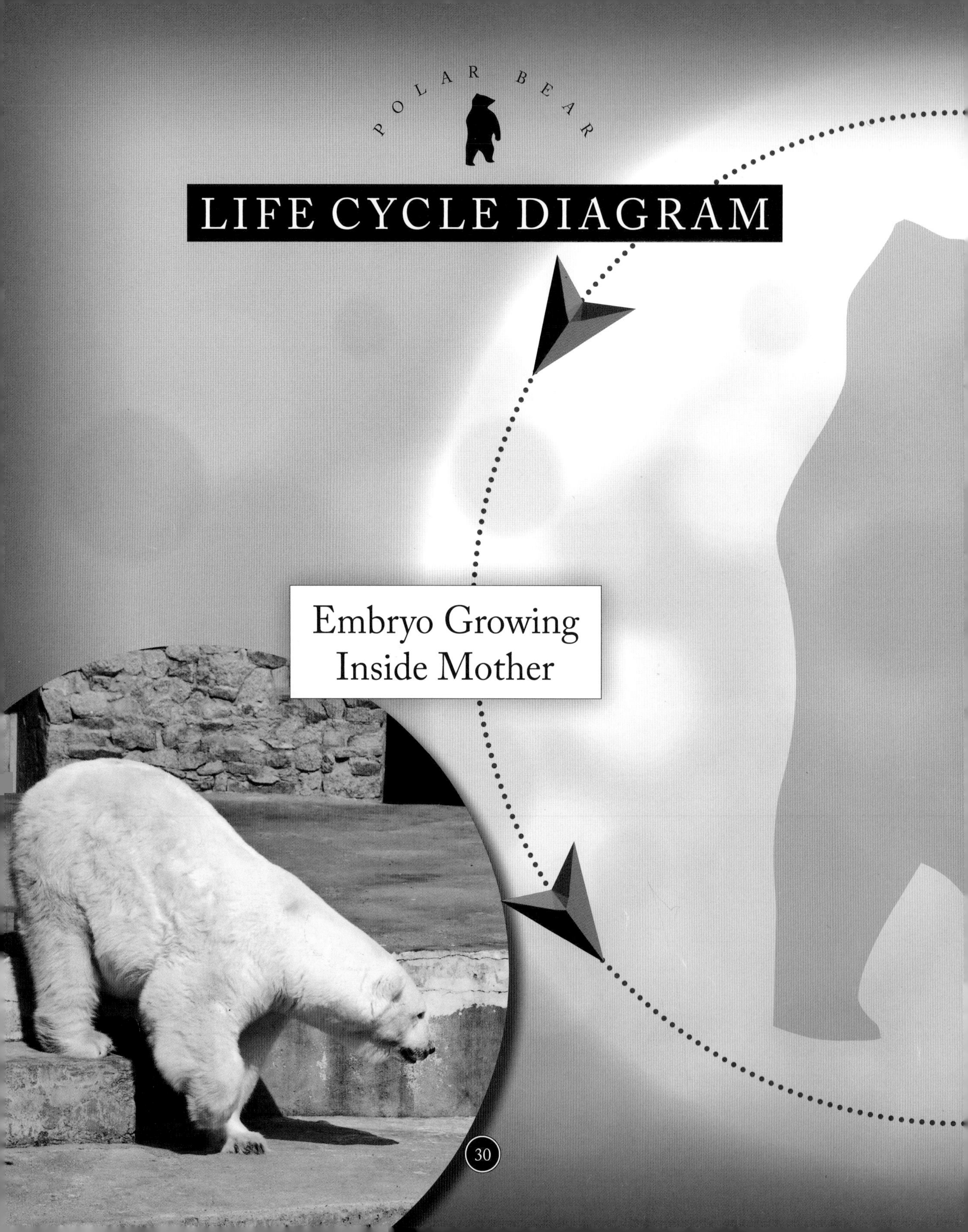
POLAR BEAR
LIFE CYCLE DIAGRAM
Embryo Growing
Inside Mother

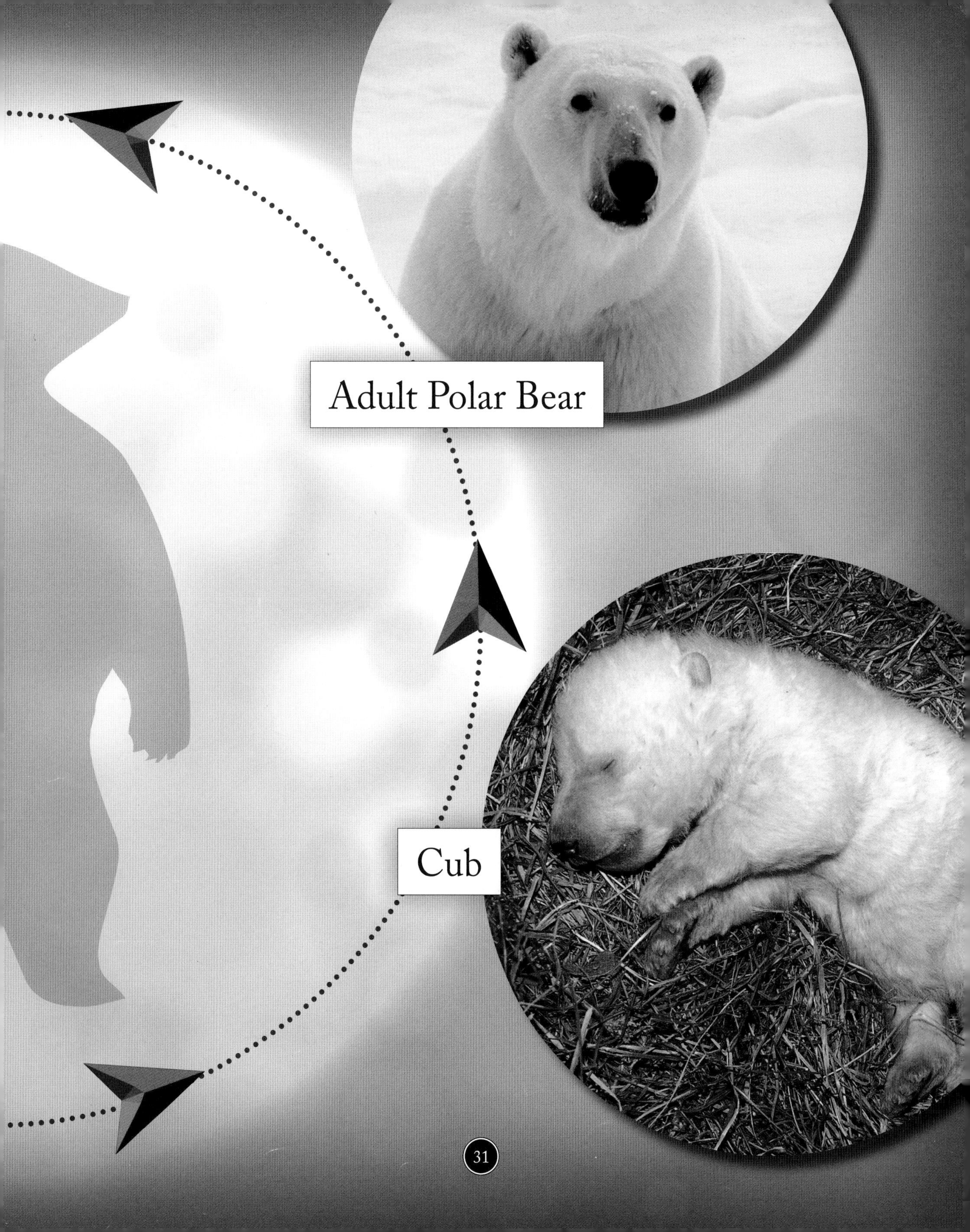
Adult Polar Bear
Cub

Web Sites

Visit our Web site for links about the life cycle of a polar bear: **childsworld.com/links**

Note to Parents, Teachers, and Librarians: We routinely verify our Web links to make sure they are safe and active sites. So encourage your readers to check them out!

Books

Hatkoff, Craig, Juliana Hatkoff, Isabella Hatkoff, and Gerald R. Uhlich. *Knut: How One Little Polar Bear Captivated the World.* New York: Scholastic, 2007.

Miller, Heather. *This Is Your Life Cycle.* New York: Clarion Books, 2008.

Reilly, Kathleen M. *Explore Life Cycles! 25 Great Projects, Activities, Experiments.* White River Junction, VT: Nomad Press, 2011.

Glossary

blubber (BLUH-bur): Blubber is thick body fat. Blubber helps keep a polar bear warm in the Arctic.

camouflage (KAM-uh-flahzh): Camouflage is the coloring and markings that allow an animal to blend in with its surroundings. A polar bear's camouflage helps it sneak up on prey.

den (DEN): A den is a space under ice, snow, rocks, or soil that shelters an animal. A mother polar bear digs a den when she is preparing to have cubs.

embryo (EM-bree-oh): An embryo is an organism in the early stages of growth. A polar bear embryo grows and changes for six to nine months inside the mother.

hibernation (hye-bur-NAY-shun): Hibernation is a state of very deep sleep, with slowed breathing and heartbeat. Pregnant polar bears do not go into hibernation, but they do sleep on and off in their winter dens.

mammals (MAM-uhlz): Mammals are warm-blooded animals with hair or fur that make milk for their babies. Polar bears are mammals.

nurse (NURSS): To nurse is to feed a young animal with milk from its mother's body. Polar bear mothers nurse their cubs to give them the nutrition they need.

predators (PRED-uh-turs): Predators are animals that hunt and eat other animals. Polar bears are among the largest predators on land.

pregnant (PREG-nunt): A female is pregnant when she has an embryo or fetus inside her womb. A pregnant female polar bear eats a lot to store up energy and fat.

prey (pray): Prey is an animal that is hunted by another for food. Polar bears catch prey with their strong paws.

reproduces (ree-pruh-DOOS-ez): If an animal or plant reproduces, it produces offspring. A polar bear pair reproduces and makes young cubs.

Index